This book belongs to

_____

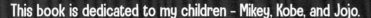

Ambitious Ninja

Pictures by
Jelena Stupar

By Mary Nhin

I was feeling down.

Everything I had tried to achieve lately had failed, and I couldn't understand why.

I wished there was a better way to get what I wanted.

One day, my friend, Passionate Ninja, found me sitting on the floor. I wasn't in a good mood.

Passionate Ninja explained, "There are process goals, performance goals, and outcome goals."

I was a little confused.

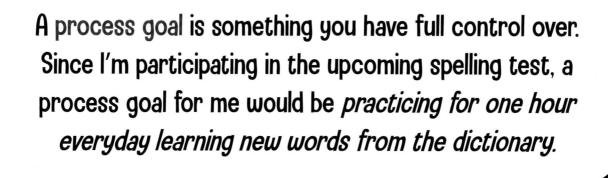

Don't forget... Outcome goals are:

NOT CONTROLLABLE

As soon as I got home, I went over what I learned with my parents. I drew it on the board so it would help them understand.

BLACK BELT

BROWN BELT

RED BELT

PURPLE BELT

BLUE BELT

GREEN BELT

ORANGE BELT

YELLOW BELT

WHITE BELT

The last goal I've created is an outcome goal. I want to get my purple belt! I don't have control over this but if I work really hard on the last two goals, I believe I can achieve it.

Over the next few months, I worked hard at all my goals.
I remembered my commitment to myself and I kept up
the practices and the sparring everyday.

Then one afternoon, my karate teacher awarded
me a purple belt. I was so happy!

Passionate Ninja had just won the Spelling Bee so we celebrated with ice cream!

Remembering P.P.O. could be your secret weapon in achieving your goals.

PROCESS

Please visit us at ninjalifehacks.tv to check out our box sets!

 @marynhin   @GrowGrit
#NinjaLifeHacks

 Mary Nhin   Ninja Life Hacks

 Ninja Life Hacks